Free Verse Editions
Edited by Jon Thompson

An Image Not a Book

Kylan Rice

Parlor Press
Anderson, South Carolina
www.parlorpress.com

Parlor Press LLC, Anderson, South Carolina, 29621

Printed in the United States of America
S A N: 2 5 4 - 8 8 7 9

Library of Congress Cataloging-in-Publication Data

Names: Rice, Kylan, author.
Title: An image not a book / Kylan Rice.
Description: Anderson, South Carolina : Parlor Press, 2024. | Series:
Free verse editions | Summary: "An account of relearning how to
dwell in this world (the only world there is) in the aftermath of a
catastrophe"-- Provided by publisher.
Identifiers: LCCN 2024035080 (print) | LCCN 2024035081 (eb-
ook) | ISBN 9781643174365 (paperback) | ISBN 9781643174372
(pdf) | ISBN 9781643174389 (epub) Subjects: LCGFT: Poetry.
Classification: LCC PS3618.I2996 I43 2024 (print) | LCC
PS3618.I2996 (ebook) | DDC 811/.6--dc23/eng/20240802
LC record available at https://lccn.loc.gov/2024035080
LC ebook record available at https://lccn.loc.gov/2024035081

978-1-64317-436-5 (paperback)
978-1-64317-437-2 (pdf)
978-1-64317-438-9 (ePub)

2 3 4 5

Front cover image: "Temple at Baalbec: Sheet of Sketches of Columns"
by James Bruce (1730–1794). Public domain. Yale Center for British
Art, Paul Mellon Collection
Cover design by Kylan Rice.

Parlor Press, LLC is an independent publisher of scholarly and trade
titles in print and multimedia formats. This book is available in
paperback and ebook formats from Parlor Press on the World Wide Web
at https://www.parlorpress.com or through online and brick-and-mortar
bookstores. For submission information or to find out about Parlor Press
publications, write to Parlor Press, 3015 Brackenberry Drive, Anderson,
South Carolina, 29621, or email editor@parlorpress.com.

Contents

Contents

for my friends

I seek an image, not a book.

—W. B. Yeats, "Ego Dominus Tuus"

0

Epithalamium

after Donald Revell

Invited to a banquet in a field, I am the only one
to flatten grass or muddy creek, so that the path I take is obvious
and shorter than I thought. The others here I know. My brother
holds a friend's new son, eyes darker than they'll be
a month from now, not offering to let me hold him too,
and I do not think to ask. The speech

I'm here to give includes the story of a family driving through
some trees one shining day. The image isn't mine, but I'll tell it
like it is, as if I felt it too, bound all at once to those I love
by shared speed and the brightness
of the road. Or maybe it's

the road I love. I am here to try to tell you
what I love. The sheets of irrigation ice from watersheds. The nearby
ditch it freezes in, routed first through half a dozen reservoirs
before it reddens the hand that lifts
and lets it fall. A dream is shallow, only deep
as I can reach, and brought with me each morning
bringing nothing back except this empty-handedness, the hand
cupped as it might to hold a neck upright
or carry water dark with shadow where I kneel, look down,
see past it to the bottom, there
                              to what is gold and flecked
          and when I cross
                    will shift beneath my step.

0

Garland

[helen]

what to the eye is green
was forced
a bud   a diamond
of extreme pressure, that barest pressed release
of vows a flower is   you fear
all month it is a false spring, snows
for sure will rout
the early garlanding
you would not have it come so easily
all form a form of branching
or deferral, a fruitful letting-go
-unsaid   you to Nags Head
I to the gulf, the easily breached
levees   the recession of
a different feeling   a poem
holds nothing together
but is instead a study in the hand, a hand inside a book
of hands and how
they may be drawn
the hardest part to render
to hold out and let be held
on a scramble to the shoreline
with nothing else to do
but haul in driftwood, washed-up forest, and build a lean-to
the makeshift structure of an afternoon
no ships
no deeds
          tide to the thigh
returning the same

[catie]

the wrong thought melts   the way things aren't
is snow, the runoff makes the heart
or valley green again   explain to me
what we are falling through, disrupting nothing, as water
in a temporary pool
accepts a certain span
of light into itself, but skims some off, dross
or scum, the range reflects
a kneeler's face, unconscious it is blind Eros
with a bow in hand who stands behind him—
                                  except it doesn't feel
like falling   you cup my inner ear, a bruisable
fruit in your palm, ripe
for the words you would speak to have me
say back to you
in the manner of a prayer
to summon you, who are not here—   held there
against this hurtling, at rest in the bowstring's blur
is it a name
you want   say it   is it
Catie, who last night dreamt of us
together reading poems, burning sage
that she and David gathered on his family's land in Steamboat
and tied for each of us with string, the burning of which once dry
will purify a room, for in every poem
is a demon
or one who appears unasked
or was asked in all but words: make of my heart
a green place, sedge
you can sink to your hip in

[alisa]

the speech of friends
        who came and stayed
that spring that filled
        with temporary ponds
in thickened fields
        was brightness that appears
before an angel says its name

                I put it flat
        to not pass through
                the blade the eye is held
                up to that wind-serrated
            surface, holding
back, not entering, not slid in
then out again,
then re-emerging, bather for a breath
that wrecks reflection
wherever it might form, the upper world
internalized as lower
                a green panic
settles in in knee-deep weeds, a restlessness
that spreads, the deepening
hunger of a whole day spent in water
or if not in
        it, near, and looking
    in
            and not quite
joining them

[colin]

going after a rat snake
he vanishes into the interface
of tender unbent reed
that rises to the waist between
the slope and muddy stream
I am in this poem
       to the extent that earlier I
       showed him my knife
       in view of the desire that he said he had
       (were he ever one to hunt)
       to drop from above on an unmindful deer
       and take it with a blade,
       the wound unmediated
       by the impersonal distances
       interposed by compound
       bow or laser
       sight   his object
with the snake neither capture
nor conscious
torture, but commitment instead
to thoughtless pursuits   a reprieve from thinking
this could be part of a poem,
but also knowing that it's not enough
to know what you are doing
while you're doing it, a serpent
swallowing itself   to achieve
       instead a letting-be that means
       (unintuitively)
       to grip by the base
       of the occipital bone, where the brainstem ends,
       and carry it back
       so that I, on the path, less hip-high
       in softstem bulrush and blue flag
       iris, can also see
       have it brought close to me
                   half-coiled in his hand

[poem after reading the first eight tercets of canto x of the Paradiso]

this side of the wisteria
                    wetted to the windshield, I watch the light
backscattering
          through particles remaining
          of the day, the day's particulars, the lantern-shaped
take-out box
in a spring storm strewn parking lot
at evening knowing no description of
a single object is enough
                    to bring us close

for there are only points or periods
                              of intersect
at which one motion and another cross
not one soul
          but a garland of them
not the apple
but the apple in your hand
          is the definite, inwoven passion   a holding
in tension
                    the strain
of assembly, the extent
of what I can summon   to reconstruct
a whole fruit having
barely tasted it
               but thinking love is bright
enough to constitute the rest
a third essence   gold chased
                         into every mote of air
a thickness as of pollen
          a scattering as of having
                         had nothing to do with it
yet strewn with such perfection
that to look upon it
is to be also seized by love

[anyte]

                          so in a wind rising
                 so too your voice as if a voice
from shore, an axis in
the spindrift of this
instant of articulation, the articulation
                          of your wrist
with respect
                          to the distance between us
how else approach except in saying
                          I am about to approach
when from the air
                 there flowers a wrist
as from an axle star, an asterisk that indicates
an openness, a cross
                 -roads near the orchard in the sea-mist this
page is
         is
                          this, then, the closest that I get
to encounter, this enclosure
                 of the hand around a piece of fruit
tired though I am
         of thinking fruit
                 when I would think the hand, its technical
         intelligence, as that which thinks
the face, the mouth
made suppler the more precise
its needs, its noises, asking, then, like the saint
who would fix the instant
                          catch its glory:
                 "can my hand do this,
         or does the hand of my mouth
by its little words effect
                 so great a thing"
how else hold
your image dear
                 except in the mouth
                          your name half-said, shaping it
as "even the gods' plans
         are shaped by another?"

[a garland of souls]

not in my voice but still one heard
inside the amplifying medium of ridge and crest that forms the face: *who said*
I wanted this
　　　　at all, to be
　　　　　　in here
　　　　　　　　in any way
　　　　　among this numbered garland
I am not the hairs
　　　　　of light around my body
you think you
glorify
　　　　　　　　—but this, too, even this attempt
at an apology, admitting yes I know I have no place
to speak for you in essence is desire for a deeper form
of chorus singing
deeds and names Ezekiel

　　　　　　　　who "leads to where all plenty is"　　Helen
hooking her dog Echo to her waist　　and Carly
trims a dark cake half with lavender
　　　　　　　　　　half with inedible sprigs
and warns us what she's done, not all of this

is good to eat, you are fed
　　　　　　　　within a narrow range, your stomach the size
of a fist, your fist the limit
of your grip, an open hand
　　　　　　　　the extent you can relax, cast the uneaten portion
across a pond
or in a crevice in the earth, some hole
　　　　　　　　that is not your mouth

[our friend elpenor]

a friend is one

        who buries you

in one world

        so you can be
        more fully in the other

[echo]

                    the ruin I have read   is in the I
-beam bent like light refracting underneath
                        the weight of its collapse a shaft
that passes through the curvature
of eye the mind then
                  rights   rebuilds the image
of an uninverted world, what overarches in
                            reality, is not without
its own integrity despite the fact
that openness is now where there should be a roof

                      above a former packing room
at the Holt-Tabardrey mill, small grass
            in a loam of rotted carpet where I walk
with you, apologizing
            for one thing when I should for another
not for bringing you here
                  where the concrete might give way beneath us
            but instead for trying to make a life
                  where life would make itself, apart from me, a flowering
where rafters fall

                  we bend beneath them, slip again
behind the chainlink
and the warning signs,
                  departing less because we have no share
                in this self-devouring
of water, glass, and stone
and more because your dog is waiting for us in the car
                  and though our small abandonment is justified
by the day's coolness
                and the windows left a little open
when we return we find she has been circled
from the outside by a ring

of kids who live in the vicinity
shocked at her size, o
white bear in the back seat, each
approaching,
bringing faces to the glass
breathing on that surface
under which your animal is held, like breath,
not mine to release.

[eros / eris]

                        every spring more obsolete,
the ruined mill beside the Haw
more innerly wrecked, less pervious
to trespass, working
in between the beams of half-collapse and bent
aluminum, now garlanded
with years of river-heat and green involvement
                                    you just need
to enter it
              they tell me   nothing
holds you back, the poet
was wrong, there is no meadow
              of permission where all architectures
fall, you wreath
what you can, and when, not waiting, gather
to your breast the inter
-twinable varieties
              of weed and ground-leaf weave
them in a crown, not holding
              all apart so carefully, the world
is a crumple around you, it comes
toward you not you
                        to it don't make this
so difficult, a ring is simply fitted
to a finger, a wedding
without thinking, greetings, relations, debts and credits, a little
humming half-remembered
song recalling song
is less than fatal
less than organizing
                        heaven into rose, petals into thrones, who sits
to whose left, Peter, Anne, and facing Adam
Helen sits at folding tables on the lawn
laid with coleslaw, paper plates, boxed wine
in plastic cups at dusk
                        a temporary setting

a disposable arrangement
the pages of a loose-bound book
that all but blow in wind apart
as a candle is breathed,
     suddenly, out
   so close to the mouth

0

Fidelity

Here in plain view at another wreck, the pillared brick
and fallen roof
                    of the Fourth Street school,
the local drivers slow
to throw us shade. Defenseless in the knowledge
that we don't belong, our shadows
                              lengthen in the absence of an outwork
or embankment, hands held up to form a brow
and keep, in the language of
                    the polymath, *the pupilla*
plump and fair, and not contracted or shrunk
as in light and vagrant vision: security
                              against my own eye's
wandering—

Back on the freeway, bound
                    for Nags Head and the ceaseless
shaping of the dunes at Jockey's Ridge, you say you hope
I'd leave
          if ever I lost feeling, or felt
                              redistributed a weight,
shallow-footed on our climb to the crest, trying to come up
with a theory of sand, maybe everything
                    started as a solid body, and this
was its disarticulate attrition, kicked up
                              in the wind, blinded, if
only briefly,
          as we stagger against it, each step less straight
-forwardly consequent, adding less
                              to the overall
shift than we thought, thinking
                    what is left
will not be left
          unswept for long—

Catabasis

A sea-oat is a stylus. In wind it's bent
and practices a shallow alphabet in grains of dune-sand difficult
   to find my footing in, the shifting terraces
like temple steps I dream disintegrate
   beneath me as I try to reach the altar at the top. The crest
and overlook. The myrtles in the ravine dropping
   toward the bay, no ships in that distance. Neither pythoness
nor crisis, nothing
   burning on the beach. Language

is a dried-out myrtle leaf that mutters circles wind
in minutes will erase. The quiet hiss of sand
   against the pages of the book I've brought with me
to read, Euripides, whose Helen
   has been faithful all these years. All this work, this
razing-to-the-ground, for just a cloud
   of breathing air. An image

that assumes my name and fucks and fights on my behalf.
It was not me, I like to think. I am not
   the poems that I write. The alphabet I lightly let
replace my life. The open book fills up with cool clean grains
   as I watch dancers in the distant dunes, in white gowns
wearing helmets, moving to no music for a camera crew.
   Two priestesses. As far away as dream. A dried-out
feeling like I am the image and in Egypt
   somewhere I have kept my promises. Have wanted to.
Have had no eyes
                    for anyone but you.

Helen

And in the thick still morning heat I think how far it is,
what we might share, this state you love, the pines in cloud
forever, laths of vacant huts in disrepair and wild carrot
in the fields, infinity, the mind surging forward ahead
of itself, plunging into thickets, coppice, time too slow
to accommodate desire, and so desire eats itself, impatient,
single berry, blackcurrant, foraging this bent-thorn syntax
for whatever sweetness it might hide, our bleeding knees
and shins from wading in too deep too quick like quickened
breath that catches, tears, turns ragged on an iron trilling
nail-in-air, needs mending now, is mended now, the now
a form of constant stitchery, a fate-thread woven in and in
instead of cut, how rare in fact an ending is, how shallow
every wound, continuance incessantly I think how long
can it go on like this, the answer is infinity, or months,
a few days more, a summer more apart than spent together,

more a hint of touch, your scent on me, than touch
itself, in every nude in Europe seeing you, the Aphrodite
in the hall of the Praetorian where fragments of a statue
of an ancient guard are on display, his arm, his mace,
Love resting in a room where all defensiveness has been
dismembered, small blue flowers spilling down the high
stone wall outside, *violence his head forever* is a line
that I have read and in the words perceived myself, my own
dismemberment, except in body I am whole, unharmed,
in fact untouched by you, the denim thick between us,
hands among the garments we appraise together in the mall
my first day home, the afternoon in atriums a pretext
to be close to you, despite the guardedness and distance
that we interpose, those distances we love, the piedmont
woods, the humid flatstone ridges fledged with east pine
to the coast we lift our faces toward instead of toward

each other, shy if not ashamed, unsure, borne far
from who we thought we were, in mists, as if by gods
who carry us away and leave behind our images,
autonomous but minus us, two pseudo-Helens formed
as clouds are formed, by moisture gathering around
the dust-motes stirred as horses circle iron-shod
in front of gates that haven't fallen yet, *a motion heaving
earth into air,* the air becoming earth, a burial I breathe
when I breathe in your scent, forgetting all my promises
as do the dead, the mind a narrow creek that fills with fog
at dusk, what family was, what niece, what sister named
sonata, little phrase or tune reminding me of memory,
what memory was like, a digging-up-of-images
from when my life was not your life, enthralled, a child
touching glass at the aquarium, as if to reach the pinecone
-fish, translucent bracts like facets of a shard of quartz

with dirt still in its ridges, little clod or cumulus
inside an earthen sea, the whorl of oil left when my niece
walks away to look at marbled hatchet fish reminding me
that there is still at least this thickness keeping us
from ocean, underworld, from pinecone, pine, a difference
that the imagist obscures by writing to the waters *whirl*
your pointed pines / and cover us with pools of fir, as if the land
was also wave and foam, the outer spending of a force
that ends with its refinement as a long swift hush,
a white flung shroud that comes to rest, dragged
through the air by angels hastening to hide our nakedness
in death, a little interval, like shallow breath, between
the drifting linen and the dark low cloud of pubic hair
in Bouguereau's *Egalité,* all horizontals, proneness,
aching in the groin at Nags Head where I find
a dead deer salt-clean in the sand, its stomach eaten out,

and bend to take a picture with my phone, an image
is what's left, the shade, the shadow on the inner thigh
in sinking light, as if desire for the world means rendering
its meanest detail, joint and sinew, the object in the image
hard to tell apart from my desire for it, deer-shaped cloud
that eats itself, is now nowhere on earth, the nowhere
-now that is another's bed, it has no root, no olive-sprig
of memory, nor eucalyptus pip to hold inside my fist
as if it were a coin, a ferry-fee to finally return, recalling
cottonwoods in spring, the rushes near the creek,
an anabasis is a military turning from the shore to march
back inland, where all metal loosens soft enough to be
reshaped into a tool to work the earth, find quartz in new
-plowed fields, and use the cloudy stones as homely
paperweights to keep the pages of an art-book open
to a painting of a landscape lifted in the air, *Terres labourées,*

serene, the world at last without desire, without under
-world, no pull of gravity, or pulled, on wings,
a sycamore seed, a little spinning violence slowing
its descent, the mind's, to earth, a hundred quiet circles
in the air, *the simplest shape that I can think to mark
this feeling*, infinite, but not, I know, for long, never
long without a longing and its opposite, fidelity,
to finitude, to noun, a cow-eye made of stone, a heifer
carved into a fragment of a frieze that shows procession
to a sacrifice, the figures interlinked, the flower-girls,
the chariots, like clauses in a broken sentence threaded
to unfold a worship scene, what worshipping was like,
a peplos woven to array the statue of a marriage-god,
the god of two and two and dauncing, levity, the joy
of knowing who will bury you, and put your name
in rock so that it can't be moved, and will not drift,
will not, like sea-spray, shatter in the sun above
a bow of swart pine turned against the swell, bound
for a land you haven't seen in years so why is it
you weep the goddess asks why weepest thou who art
so gifted, it is infinite inside the hut, your distance is
your dwelling-place, and fate is laths and lintel-beams
and nails-in-air that tear your blood and leave it
hanging there, a red thread in a labyrinth flesh is
self spelled backwards plus an h, the breath you take
before you turn, at last,
                        if also empty-handed, heartsick,
home.

Fidelity

Wind, too light
                to impel pebble, shored fragment
of wet-red shell, but driven
                            enough to flute and ridge
the sand
            around what's been
                                heavier strewn: was this

what you kept trying to tell me? Think

smaller. Even the light

is obdurate, has its
resistances, which is
                to say that threshold
past which it must be
                    picked up, and must, by as much
necessity,
            be put down.

Nothing has changed, I keep

repeating. We are

who we were. Nothing is

as heavy as

could easily be thought. Which is the worse
                thought:
                            that there has been no impact
or that that impact
has been too light, too easily

withered: rose
                on its stem, insupportable
feeling of

life as it could be, if not
easy, then
spindrift, determinedly
tossed off, less a crest
than what comes after, that gentle
taking back
of what rose
then broke against the barrier.

Anabasis

                                        with loss of you there is
at last no other   option / at dusk the creek suppressed
in matted swale, star   -chickweed in its final flowering,
poor in world but all   that's left of petal-white as day
-light sinks the sunkenness   of biomass beneath itself
exhaling heavy breadth of sloe & silicate, a thickness
in the air unearthed with less & less   of sun, shéer
plód it is to breathe this   density my two lungs crudded
steel-toe in meadow mud no other   waiting there for me

among the milkweed spurred   to desiccate & split, a
softness spilling out / if only it were possible to make
the mind like that, tough   head horn-burst   memories
a shallow breath could disengage each   breath a dis-
engagement from the earth that comes again to rest, not
at last borne far, smokefall of remembering   how limited
the lung how modest the line what little of the world
it can actually hold   a fieldmouse held loose

inside a shirt bites through the linen   to the skin the poet
says the other is, says you   is / a saying-you to give you
weight as lower light makes earth of air   my laboring
to suck with every o a shovelful, a boot   -thrust blade
through roots & bedded silt in ancient creek it's hard
to say if I am burying or digging up each next breath un-
subtracting depth the last breath   dowsed with trachea
& doubled lung the body bent a why   -shaped witching

rod above this page, the ʌ   in ˈsɪʌən or sillion the shine
of dirt upturned in lines that only spade   a little at a time
in hopes of turning up with bull   -tongue plow a sunken
noʌ, destroying   buried nests of fieldmice the cloth a poem
is can't hold this   little of the world & not   release,
the turn in breath a bite I   give myself a you a wound I
soon forget how sharp it was, this loss   that only leaves
a sediment, the further   subsidence of long-dead

thicket-weed, a compensating density where I had hoped

to find a branching opening / an empty o addressed to no
one burrowing   a hole inside the air I harrow now with
either/or as if there were   some other
                                        world to cut my losses in

0

levity

and yet the heart   is still
less hardened than this morning's   robin, unsplittable
weight. for once to not internalize, nor take so heavily
what is already   a point of total density, the juniper
bent   less   around the gram   of song
-breast than a black hole little

                                        ousia little more
-than-meets-   the-eye   -gone-god-white in the husk-
light. the light like chaff. its   lightness
has to do with mass. with settling   for less
and less. increasingly. the increase in a sack   as if of
grain I groan beneath. the heft, all   -gathering,
this zeroing   in. the piercing thistle-sting it ends in,
everything with crown inviting

                                        touch, my blood
-gemmed thumb at first   less wound than source
of   dumbness, quiet unserious

                                        interest, split
second of *that wasn't*

                                        so bad as

synapse, late
                -flown choros,

                                catches, breathless,

up

.:)

rage is also prone to structure. being gotten hold of. rod
that enters thru the cheek   transects left hemisphere
and exits frontal bone   also flowers. bursts,
but into several interlayered surfaces. thousand-petald
war-lily. orderly   chord and tangent   pike and lower
jaw, blade at its angle   of deflected incidence, non-
event of what was thought   would this time stay
transfixed. really pierced.   a robin's breast
by thorn, christ's singer.   or an atmosphere's
eternal red, ammonium   irradiated, ancient
hypercane, jovian
                    blemish,   wood-knot in a plank of
winter-cherry   for a temple, hardening   of pulse
into a fitting rhythm. all veins
                    tight with it. pushed to the surface, all
but breaking into air. open to it. walls unfallen under
aerial campaign, carpet of fire   cool to the cheek, less
unmoving than unmoved.   whose head spins
with the stillness of a chopper's blur. a hovering in self
              -created vacuum,   bluestem
grasses flattened under
                        -neath this airy
                                    radius. endless
rehash how
              it could   (could it)
have happened.   or how it could
not
        not. not
              be trumpeted. brass
                                    calyx. sheath
                        or shield
that lark
              -splits, silver
                              worlds roll out

.:)

it burns slower what was thought of   highly, structured.
the more ornate the less   it's pervious to fever. cedars
only blackened. back of every leaf   a darker leaf, law
of shade   retreated to to   speak (*o*   , *speak,*   *shade*
.). but the lesson is the worlds   don't crash through.
there is just the one   I love. if anything the pressure
of an upper realm below. less bursting in
               than bulge. fruit   in a shirtfront   .:) planet
in a pocket of it   -self that light   drops in
and dies into the exosphere as day. the light's
                       too-lightness
(and my love's.). the day after   day of it. years
it seems   of spring. the world unburning. untouched
image. nothing   to be done about its all
-consuming aureole. deathless   god of the apple-core.
of what is
          yet to be consumed.   whole precincts of
the temple. wasps in the eaves.   honey and amber in
flecks on the leaves.   even fish inside the sanctuary
pond are   ambiciliate,
                 armored   on both sides
as everywhere shines
              christ's unpierceable
          three-eyed beam

.:)

structure   as a form of rage itself. atria
and corridors. airiness   of vault
the outcome. all speech   echoes
as if lightly spoken. no light step below   not building
in the upper reaches into   onslaught, storming   host, visored
order of thrones.   given over to this vision in
which nothing is   actually seen. what actually is
a fucking death   -hyacinth. almond
petals versus actual memory.   the endless strewing of
which from a rod   whose blossoms prove
who gets priesthood. hieratic ephod. called hierophant
even by my friends. the marrier if not
                              the merrier
                                        of them.
if not light   -hearted then their structurer.   up-
gatherer of what is then less easily   let go of. lost
touch with. un-with
                      -ering garland.   how unbreachable
the palisades by spring tides   immovable
the whirligigs
                      by spring storms   whatever toiling
there is
          self-   levied and so also self   -ground-
to-a-halt. stopped.   in its tracks. destroyer given
pause. the ear the thing (if   anything)
                                        cocked

.:)

as gun-heavy. as   sunken as
a trigger is depressed   in series is this
trigger   -happiness. this mindless   firing
of synapses an index   finger's leaden
pressure is. ungentle   lightless deixis. the hand
itself a fire hiding   more in shadow than it shows. this
meager apocalypse. rent veil   of what was
barely there between us. collapse of worlds for what. what
clarity or field   of vision. flame-tipped glittering
with dew the lamb's   -ear blackening
the hand thrust into it. thought
                          myself stoic to withstand
that tenderness
              to touch. burning if not
                              in this then in
twenty-fold dimensions.   if not this
then that. every flower spinning   on its double axis, pollen
is a qubit, a zero and a one that can't   self-cancel.
that just gets
              denser. increasingly coded. only legible
with *lights* and *perfections*, with   *urim* and *thummim*. this
hiero   -gamete, archy   -spore. spore
that structure is. that hut   on field's edge. that pasture-
militance that knowing
                      -what-I'm-doing
is, its nettle
            -technics /   risks. what
                          bitterness. and all
for this. this first
                shallow upward flight of stairs. its
weed-cracked adamant.
                      as christ cracked world
and let the other in

35

.:)

life in this world   the other's catastrophe. the other
turned against. dis   -armed. un   -faced, faced
away from. friends   are those who turn
back to bury you   properly in one world
so you can be more   fully in the other.   more all
in. in rage there is   arrival of the mouth
before the mind, wind-   torn. gut gone
through with a horn. giddied by it.   repeatedly gored.
doing it but doing it   to self. for death
if good is death   controlled. a handle
gotten on its oaken   haft. an oar thought
threshing rod   is to at last
arrive   at where   you can
turn back, gone   far enough. innerly
bloody to the elbows, outwardly   light. as all things
are, made outer. unconcealed.   lit
from within as from without. sunt lumina.   sunt's
bright un-   blunted edge. sun   -light-caught.
sharpened into thought
                                    -lessness. what else
is there to dull this on: my one
                            low thought. this
low-swung blade I   arc where wheat
                                is straight and far
            from burning shores

.:)

where desire was was edge. was wild   order. where edge was
hem or herm.   was hesitance, the circlet
not yet   cinched, the head not cinctured yet
with hyacinth, with lily-gold   and light. as gold
will gather light, so pollen cleaves   to foreleg, future
nectar, denser   over time like time
made whole, its sweetness   like meridian, the coming
singularity. all mass collapsed to form   a gram,
a calorie
             that burns as quickly as the retina
when looking at the sun. the eye   run through
like democoon   with pike, the darkness flooding
in is sugar making
          medicine go down. the health it is
     to see,
to look up
      at the serpent, icon
          made of bronze. image
as of hermes   at the crossways
        by the sea-shore, god
of boundary, laws of edge of acreage. freehold. forms
of property whose end
       will be millennium
          the coming
          absolute
community. complete transparency   of earth a sea
of glass and fire. pressurized
         to coesite and garnet. poly-
hedral hive   of light, everywhere
refracting
      into rainbow. broken
         into hierarchy. as heart
is hardened paradise
      is structural.   as rose
is multifoliate
       and scentless un-
         less crushed. wave

-length gnashed. by light
                    let.
                                as blood by nick
of time a petal is
                    released. too
                                        built up. too
humorous. silly
                                with it. feverish
visions. the needed little
                                harms. the needed
littleness
                    of spurt. good light
                                -headedness. room
for once the spinning thing. I
                                for once untoiling.
uncoiling
                    on an axis like
                                the inflorescence of
a wet black bough

.:)

the stone   to stone   a river is in its descent.
bough over bough. forests upon forests   hung. the world
as it was known to worlds as mists   disperse.
by noon the earths   have blackened out the sun.
as water-bugs will dimple river -bed with shadow where
the foot indents. the lens it is to step. as light thru lens
incinerates. as seed   is focused heat. point
where gyres inter   -clypse or prick.   drill in. droplet
after droplet
               fracking granite   into clast. fissure and gas
the oracle inhales whose head   is light. is fire in
the hole. the earth
                    rent gently

                                        for this
profit-harmless
               sip. this usufructed gram
                              of dew. the burning
unconsumes. cerebral   flaming in a vacuum. thought
is things
                    remaining as they are, wavering
hiero-   glyph of   wood thrush,
dusk. gypsum   -dusted moth-wing.   our love's
lightness. its bent
                              step shines
black thru clarity
                    to bed. to sediment. what comes light
to rest, shallow
               breath who breathed
                              in heavily
honey and milk
               and spurt
                              through sinuses
who laughed
               at anvil
                    fallen from the sky. its sudden
unconcealment. denser
                    middle of the air

39

                              a wing-beat is. is being

bludgeoned. breast's
                white   feather
                                              braining-
                                                    in in

        being
                    so caught up. so
up
            beat

.:)

the zero thought   it took to get
this   stemless seepage through
a shirtfront. fruitlessness   of pressure self
-applied. its zero   good. good   o. little hole
the mouth makes in this   afferent interval. this being
dawned on. daylight   thought is. noon
of thought of wounds that wholeness   preexists. groundless
o or orb. a bubble   blown. lucent tinctured gaseous
planet. all   wobbling atmosphere.
the airy green   preceding world   -collapse. another one
blown after it   for fun. world   on world
whose gentle gravities
                    will self
                        -annihilate. will lightly
sink
                            to lawn. bristling
mint. clover-bladed   ground or *grund*   we soberly
descend to
                    breeze
                            -dropped
                            in a sudden
zero of exhilaration. gauge
                    invariance and symmetry. force
that order is. ionic
                compound columns
                        in the temple, eye
or umbel. unsimple
                    leaf. bipinnate or phyllo
-tactic to a common axis, axle, spinless
                            particle or lily
of the field. effortless
                    twenty-fold dimensioning
a flower is. its perfect
                    stasis. crystal. beryl. spodumene or
spodium *who knows*
                why bone ash
        stancheth

41

bleeding it is written

in a poem called the Lily

of Medicine. the flower

of sanity. bone

where wound was

flourishing. where wound

was rose. now risen

whole. hole-

handed. empty

-headed. perforate

third eye where

the blood had built. where humor was

is sight. is foxtails

in the sunlight. pool towels

drying on the railing

overnight. dog bark

muffled behind glass. arcs of water opal

-flung in air

by sprinkler, spurts of

coral-silver world

on world that this

world is

Redux (for E)

after Gustave Caillebotte's "The Floor Scrapers"

that shore, torn to, turned back, tar   on my hands,
terns above the headlands where you never were you
laid your head by mine inside   a tent on the beach
in the mind and asked   what war was that what
was it then   between us   breached, bare feet,
wet books read out loud in rain beside the creek. how
did we greet each other   then. what was thought
harmless. how close   constituted nearness
of a miss or shallowest   of graze, blood
in the sand a blade -let gem's black hardening before
the thought had time   to crystallize *I could
have made this*
         shallower, stayed
                more on the surface, light
and over-light, sheen
                of sweat, strigil to scrape
each other clean as adze
          the flooring
                in the painting
in another life that we two must have stood
                  before, its
layer after layer laid to bring   to light the labor
of taking away. the work of barely   brushing to lay
bare ground that gleams
          beneath our feet. to lessen it
to loosened
     cloud the shore
        -line made
          of grain on grain but filled
with bright clear light as from
                   a sun
        below, our aerial
atopon or instant
        in   which
            breath
               is drawn

as string
        to cheek   and tensely
                      held the less
you think
        your aim
           the nearer that
              your miss will be. the weirder
it will feel
        to walk away
              unwounded, not floored
by the brunt, groundless
              in our grievances, white pine
planks unbroken underneath
              our weight, not dropping
free, no
        other world
           to hit
                    but this

0

Shield or bee

for Dan & Danny

Instead of world   a weed the lesson was   you cannot write
a book that holds   itself together all   coherence needs a seed
of carelessness the choice   you didn't know   you made
all marriage is   a sudden hardening   to fact   the fluid in the inner
ear a stone   that listened to itself   all solidness
a gradual self   -deafening or song   obsessed with song
itself as self   -defense   a shield that I learned   to hum
a single note repeatedly   to hold inside the head as if it were
a memory where there are only images   I've never seen   the bee
of the invisible   that flowers into tangibility another student claims
as his and leaves the shield to me   its echelons in anaglyph how
commerce works how   cattle sweat how   world protects
the one who sums   it all into the surface of a bent bronze disc
then holds it up   to hide behind my gentleness the obverse of this
armor-imagery   no knowledge in reality of how
a face is crushed beneath the deftness of a pike   thrust
into it the face   remains a fact a pond   returned to tension is
a lesson in   how little harm is ever done   how little little
harms submit themselves to memory   how easy to forget
the clover-bee I killed today   the unresisting soft   slow gold
of coin embossed   with symbols of a solid state
a hero's face the obverse of   an eagle with a shield becomes
a source of randomness no human memory can generate   this
either-   or or law or   war that could go either way   the softness
of the open field a poem is the tenderness   of skin that shows
between the armor   -leaves the words   I can't remember of
the song I have to hum another student   knows by heart the ur
-sound of the honey-bee   I only know this   banging on a shield this
buzz buzz   this this   there is just this   earworm   world is

35°43′00.5″N 75°29′29.5″W

A penlight passed across the iris
is this sun in sea-mist nothing can be seen in, test
of health of vision, circumference
that self-annihilates, shrinks
into a disc of muted gold: a CD flung in mud
beside the highway, songs
inscribed a micrometer's width
apart. Compressed,
what is recorded starts to feather, tuft apart, cirrus clouds
iridophoric in the lifting fog revealing no destroyers
anchored off the coast. And through this
sudden clarity I watch you
in the looseness of your winter jacket
crossing toward me on the lawn
beside a decommissioned lighthouse,
the crystal acorn in its brain
unlit and obsolete. Not blind, the eye, but also
not glittering for once, not diffracting
as it sings the risk of your approach. All earlier
uncertainties and treacheries
burnt off, leaving what little there is to record
of the day, a windy lunch between the dunes, dolphins
in the upswell, your delight
in that sleek proximity, the joy
we like to read into the commerce of things
that were we there among them would not hurt
nor even give us second thought.

35°45′53.5″N 79°12′01.8″W

For once a meadow not in the mind. And the white tufts
therein and the torn stems past blazing at the angle
of receding light, a trailer in its midst, unhitched, and lichen
in the mesh of the c-band dish. The difference
between an image versus vision is that one of them is given
with the instantaneous reception
of a seraphim, where the blue
that it comes out of is the blue
tarpaulin roped around the Datsun in the yard. The rippling
muscle on the dog or cherubim. The radius
it turns in, or the distance-from
that gives a thing its property, poetry
that ground
you have to cross
before a risk is real. The HD
in between. That ripple in the screen. It's as if
I am actually there, all this burning
actually happening, when in reality the dogwood tree
that spreads above the propane tank
still blossoms, coldly, morning
also bringing dew
to the blackened polyester
of the cushions on the patio. How it must be. The imperceptible
collapse if not of government of confidence
in process. The thought that this is how
it must be now, now's unwithering, there is just
this, you are in it, you cannot trespass what
you cannot think yourself outside of
thought for thoughtless is the one
with shotgun saying can't you fucking read
that this is private property.

35°54′05.4″N 78°50′45.2″W

Flipped truck in the ditch.
Fog in the fields. The little it leaves
of a working day but work, where work is what is near. Where
what is near is least perfected. Most the urine
brown from being in its bottle in the sun beside the road
the mud of which if stripped of its impurities and left alone
would self-arrange to silicate, to hexagon, clear
and set so that it gathers only out of light the bluest rays,
refusing all the rest. The earth
become a crystal sea. And how easily. This slippage
into slough or splendor's rut. The war
between the limestone and acicular
in all of us a spire is the leafiness
of tabernacle stone. Its shimmering with schist as if
embedded in its matrix was a rainstorm intercut
with sun. Thus the light rains, thus pours, e lo soleills plovil, light
the first body of heaven and heaven at its outermost redounding
from its perfectness to build circumferences
within, the way a lark is split and bulb
on bulb spills out, a little flood of glass spheres made
inside the lighting fixture factory near Stirrup Iron Creek
which trickles with the opal sheen
of oil through the watergrass-aluminum amalgamate where lambs
lay down with three-eyed lion
-asps among the empty
Miller Lites that fill the watershed
transected by a business loop
on pillars overhead.

35°59'49.1"N 78°54'11.1"W

I spat out the slender oat. At which was said such bitterness
did not become me. What was there, after all, at this
late hour to renounce. The locking in had happened
and with the special force it takes to fully shut
a dented tailgate, the also-battered bed unloaded
of its rural gear then heaved and slung what could across
the stronger of two shoulders. Foxgloves
in the valley also garmented in cartridges. Everything in its right
array, splayed out, gainly apparatus of the tripod
whereon stands the barrel of a gun or bowl of visionary smoke.
The scope in which a god appears. God of target
-softness, soft but without loss of structure, rondure
not without its vigilance. The maintenance of gentleness
as though it were perimeter or rind. Thatch-eve's
mellow fruitfulness securitized. The cottage
industries and local enterprise patrolled by seventeen-year-olds
and aldermen in body vests. The smallness of the business
is a trigger to the blood. The self-containment of
a cartridge carrying the name of Hatshepsut they call
cartouche. The prenomen within. He of the sedge and of
the bee, meaning king over all, of the upper and the lower,
all-owner. Circumscriber of horizon. Of the holding in mind
of the world as tightly as I would a spring frog caught
among the grasses by the pond, sealed yet still afforded
space enough to spit the terseness of my fist. The slip
the body gives the world as world gives grip
or apprehension, knowledge twin to nervousness. Fear
is foresight said my father after sucking hard the siphon tube
that snaked into the fifty-gallon water-drum we kept
refreshed in the event of grid-collapse. He showed me how
you only had to get it started. Create with your lips around
the plastic flute an instigating vacuum. What then flowed
flowed from itself, like light or charity. You can do it too
with gas he said. Say you need the fuel. It's true that some
will fill your mouth but if you're quick to spit it out in small
amounts it will not hurt you. As he bid me try the struggle
I had cupped to show him leapt from me and vanished
in the grass we worried then to walk across
and crush the little guy.

35°53′28.6″N 79°02′26.4″W

Something less controlled instead. A truer rot, and not this gentle
desiccation, wasp detached by frost
from a cusp of its own making. And if not shaven fury
then a visionary sense of dread, a glimpse of the white domes
and clarifying tanks where shit is churned to effluent
in the sanitary labyrinth of pipes that gleam with leveled sun
between the leafless trees. "Injured beauty"
as one idea of the truth, a kind of compromise, the settling
of solids to the bottom of the stabilizing basin as an object
comes to rest inside the brain, crystal
in its liquor, now
shadowless, all one multiplex
of inner halls of light. Wherein nothing is without
its possible purities: the feather or the condom
in the slough. Or the white strips marking line or property
that flutter in the woods beside the cut
with concrete pedestals at intervals
for accessing the sewage main. In the dusk's grey
-gold you pull a ribbon from its branch and climb the manhole
of a stunted column where you show me Warrior III
then Toppling Tree, the quiet rushing
underneath you
of a buried river, the activated muscle-groups inside
your calf and thigh a counterforce
to your constrained precarity, a risk
that doesn't override your tendency to take the world
less heavily, less allowed to settle into place, floc
and biofilm, what the body has ejected self
-arranging into ribbons, zoogloeal
winding sheets that leave
the outflow purer, and if not drinkable, acceptable
in its toxicity
for watering the lawn.

Gnat brain

It must be loose the swarm   of gnats in sun
above the mud   o happy gnat o patternless
in shaft whose happiness   is agitant within a rim
of lowered light a levity   that limits its extent to breadth
and depth no looser   than a human head or shattered
visage in the sand the obsolete   remains of overreach the poem is
a witness to its ruined cold
command   an eye that fails to see by seeing only
what is dark in clarity a seed   sucked clean of sweet transparency
the plainness of a simple   *plum*   a word
I watch you say but silently to savor how
it shapes your stoneless mouth and puts in mine a pit a hollowness
inside a semi-scattered head that fills with light
and hovers bodiless above the mud   of forest acres simplified
but for a single tree we crossed the clear-cut field to stand beneath
its shade and speak   vocat   aestus in umbram shade
of what is left   the residue
of appetite   a bowl with remnants of   some shredded rhubarb
days will crystallize   to perfect cubes a fact
or facet ripening that splits
the light from light and proves   a beam is only loosely
bundled by the eye   as vividness the fruit
you ate while sitting on green carpet in the sun
-reflooded room you tell me is
your strongest winter memory and is
for me a form
of furious repair

Luminism

on crossing in front of the light from a 1080p LCD projector

Light is a field   I interrupt   inside the half-
dark of the gallery   the catacomb the image
    forms   half-blinded by a little sun
behind its lens as I glance back   a knot
    of pixel-density that's meaningless until
the dust can be seen drifting through its looser
    pasture in the air the void turned wheat
-gold flooded with a video I   breach I

    burrow through   this triple morn of red
green blue this dawn   at midnoon rising
    in the room adjacent to a wing of luminists
their gold frames filled with dark rain north
    -east storm-light from another century's
connecticut   eternity   in black waves that we

            interrupt—you   following

with sudden depth   with tunnel-dirt our
    shadows cast behind us in the midst of floating
images the unresolved   desire-knots of pine
    plus sea plus   breakers in the dark a vortex
formed in three-   dimensionality a storm
    of dust that fills as if with sun and spins
behind us as we cross   the room a stanza
    in a sonnet is   in love if love

means wanting you   to bury me one day
    beneath the pines beyond the flooded
field of light that follows when the noon
    -storm breaks at last the frame and gold
pours in like rain in sun the sun a liquid on its way
    to earth to solidness to rock turned crystal

            under pressure to relent

Axis

A burr in me the honey-stone   the sweet solidity
the axis also in the open mouth that splits what's
seen and doubles it   a crystal on a piece of paper
with a line that parallels itself   the ray on ray
of sun through forest corridors that fill with pollen
in the wind gold   cloud of random sex that moves
toward me and clarifies the rectitude of light   how
rightness is a time of day   how any bead of sweat
or cum can streak an isinglass of lemon quartz
along the inner thigh the mind   is dry and shuts
the eye like suppurated sleep you gently hold
my chin to pluck from me this spur of dream   this
topaz crust   a poem is   a surfacing to look
and see the pollen on your breast I brush and lode
the ridges of my thumb the self   an inadvertent bee
a cumulus I cannot help or cloud   of libraries
of seed   of protocol commanding me to grow more
orderly   anthologist of images the compound corymbs
in the ditch beside the uncut pines that rise beneath
a triple-tiered transceiver mast and randomize
the air with yellow media   the veils we breathe and
cannot read and fuck   in hopes of clarity   that this
might structure us this   vivid gentleness   the mouth
a lightweight prism on the page that multiplies
a single word into a hierarchy   a law where there
was only burr before now   odes and documents
and loyalty to family   a life in place the way
a grave-mound isn't made with just a basketful
of earth nor cloud without a latticework of hanging ice
that hides and shows and hides and shows the light

Satyrid

There's structure   in collapse collapse itself a cloud
of domes that build   above the interstate a state
-liness in fast   -corrupting terraces that every day
degrade from drifting barge to dis   -incorporated
wisps of rose the later that it gets the more I think
a glimpse of light in meadow-fog that falling forms
a hard hypotenuse might be enough to ground me
here   enough to prove geometry   will write itself
in air   a theorem that needs no theorist a field in mist
its own bright analyst   each lucid stone inside its brook
a problem solving for itself a cloud   of chalk erased
from slate the lesson that a poem is the wound
it also heals crossed out the faintest trace of   0 in place
of it a dark   -furred butterfly descends and comes
to rest beside my hand while writing   wounds
from air each wing-ridge rimmed with little voids
surrounded   gold and pricked   with white as if
a distant star collapsing to a point of light the mind
attempts to form a theory from a string of such
as these these pin   -prick glimpses seen throughout
a day and hardened then to gold-encircled cameos
of cosmoses that line   like eyes the edges of a span
my breathing   stirs to flight that stirs in turn the air
above my wrist a gentleness that makes me lose
all thought of wounds I learned I had   to write to lose
my memory and love instead the world unfolding right
in front of me its wing from wing arrayed with camouflage
to make me think a spotted lynx is looking back at me
a threat when in reality it kisses me o   imago o shade o
                              mother I forgot I had

Tongue-tie

after "On the Church of the Holy Martyr Polyeuctus,"
Greek Anthology, I.10

Must-lute, now-lute: a song is plucked as is
an epigram at random from a stephanus or wreath
of copied lines inscribed in stone they indicate
is there to glorify the parent of the renovator
who alone with added ell and apse did violence
to time the song a form   of chance   integrity
a glimpse   in stone a speckled bird that knows
to rest behind the eye   the ounce by ounce
a daughter is at first the fear she won't amass
the pebbles in the mouth that straighten speech
precision is a heap   of shells that teach the golden
ratio that gives its structure to the armor-home
you leave   the multi-family edifice among
the wheat-gold hills of Kennewick where cousins
emptied firearms into a bale of hay is long since
sold by now   my mother helps her mother
throw away a life's   collectibles and asks and this
and this does this have memory attached this lamb
in porcelain that hangs upon a string you randomly
accrued   a fleece with dew   the mind then
wrings into the bowl a poem is   enough to sip
the morning's path through wetted panicles
that hide the bird that knows   its silence is its best
defense   the future is secured withholding
singing's thoughtless ordering   of air that just
as soon will fall apart a narthex cut from rock
these lines were written in to prove that children
also build   assert   their presence in the world
the daughter of a friend is placed upon a zeroed
scale to see what she retained   what milk-weight
sucked her tongue un   -lasered of the minor web
that makes the mouth a future

knot of stone and song and shell

Pitkin / Column

In childhood that prophecy   that government
should hang by a thread   in the end that
string that binds   the bunch of violets that
a tender image is is   only tender as
the framer's eye that federates   without regard
for property for property said Madison is as a source
of faction   durable   all ownership   the ownership
of gun   of egg   of house   of barn   a farm
is fate and fate is fear that   what you hate is who
you are   a traitor to yourself a self   undone
or loosened by a wound I never thought I had until I
thought it there   a self   -fulfilling sore or source
of if not wellness welling up   a prophet-pit
that fills   with blood that brings
among the dead my living mother   to its edge
a memory   of how her voice sounds when she prays
at night its sudden   gravity like slower
sunken air   beside a creek   the cooling of
her flow of speech   each thought almost pulled
apart in god-time only held   together by a litany
a rhetoric   the way a country is
its rigid columns pitted   on the page unbundling
of plinth and flute   and capital   and shattering
the heads of lilies   on the temple steps the imagist I am of rift
of flaw in crystal that   precision is   its crown
                              of facets hide a fleck
of light a speck
                or seed that breaks   as from within the self
-betrayal of
          the song that listens to
                            itself and self
                              -fulfills   its prophecy a law
that loosens me
              of memory
                   of property
                        of lamb

or corn
                coral and shells   gems
and handkerchiefs   apologies
for gifts   that are not mine are not
appropriate
                for me

                                        to freely give

A vision

she took the crystal from her mouth and put it to my lips. said don't
sip   what isn't yours. dew on the hood. nectar even in the blue
middle-of-the-urn the air is. the sweetness that just forms   as sweat
of skin on skin, skin shed of its talma and plain yoke.   its quilling of
satin ribbon, netted heading. the massy fringe in folds   between us.
as a lyric sheds itself   of secondary forms. its torque of hemihedral
scalloping. down to its tersest seed   -shape. basal cube. tenderness's
pyramid. the heart's geometry   or spar that held to sun refracts
to double paths a perfect burr   of light that splits the vision
birefringent in its following from twig to   stone from stone
to straw the robin in the brain. the spasm of its song. how the body
fights against its loosening   of loop of twine around a bunch of
violets in a vase. how else maintain   this brittle foliation into gentle
matrices and ply   on ply of shiver in the fasciae of the lamb whose
tenseness gives beneath the judge's touch at show. lamb of memory,
winched and sawn from anus to the neck and splayed into a cabinet
of specimens of highest liquid   crystal resolution. a tiny plumed
aragonite. the lemon-leaf   of orpiment on quartz. opalescent
underlay of changing blue of smoke at noon from burning gathered
underbrush. the valley filled with rose and haze from which the gas
I breathe produces no hallucinations. no   optic nutting of vicinity
to corridors of light from which an osgood steps   to spit a cat's
eye from her mouth to mine. where then is it from   this bitter
stricture-gem. this struggle to say anything that hardens when it hits
the air as grain spills to the floor where it is left for gods to get. god
of the pebble and the hay. god inside   the bract. stone with storm
inside that is another name   for mind a violence
from within protecting us from violences   without. sun-flecked
blade of falling leaf that nearly nicks my eye and so there is in graze
or grace indictment. as barb is in the feather   -brain destroying ear
worm of the nursery   rhyme a memory   if not of
nothing than with nothing's sing   -song simple structure spiculae
and pinnate star that stick in wool and melt from body   heat to
unconstructed dew. glitter in the smallness of the nanometric kinks
of fleece. and soon   that flurry built to such a depth it drags
the sheep-fence down my memories   of snow released the diamond
blazes on the trees beside   the muddy trail we climbed the stillness
of the deer that looks up at the sound   of our approach, the shock

a sudden order   like an axis in the air that tilts in light and flares
along its several planes impelling us to stop and heed   the world
reduced   to just this   rapt   radius this
all-consuming vigilance of maintenance   of distance from
whatever kindness   you could show   your slightest movements
constituting   threat as much as small adjustments of the mind
adjusting to the love   that narrows it. josepha
with a rottenstone and slitting-mill.   a minor apparatus making
less and less. a shattering to bort. berry. acorn of   light it is to be
inside the diamond-box or mortar-storm of your own   shards
your self   -containment losing lamb-shape   like a cloud
that rots away   an un-remembering of simple songs
that say *and you each gentle   animal in confidence may bind
and make them follow   at your call   if you are always kind.*

Economy

Reduced to abundance. To the thought of it. Small bowl
Sight is. Right in front of me. Oats. Sparrows. How little
Love it takes. How long it takes to cross the lawn
                                or distance from the road that was
Affordable. Appropriate. The dream that we might live
Within our means. In shade the eye's precise adjustment.
The stomata also open up. Cooling units startle on and
Thrum. This

                        summer's steady losses: range of motion
In the wrist; steadiness of aim; knowledge of the more
                        specific names for flower. The river's heat
Is such that only leaving it I realize I'm cut. The ultimate
Littleness of any wound. Tiny moan a gnat makes. Swarm
                        of mouths the leaf's green seethe it is to think
Nothing of thought. Nothing of the tiny wound
A thought makes
                        more of than there is. Such that what we lost
We only thought we lost. Noon also visits the burn pit. The pit
Of every fruit eventually will be spit out. A hatred of simple tools
Is not enough; burial will not fully hide the hammer or nail.
A bucket or a cup is also how I handle it. Logic has
Its wooden haft. The work works

                        me, husbanded by husbandry.
Married to the thought there must be more. And that it must be
Complex. Intricate. Shadow-pattern from the lines
Of fruit trees that the tools lay in the grass beneath.
Spade that dug the pit to hold the blood that drew
The shade to it. The arbor's early gloom it was abandoned to.
Left to its own devices. Its working seethe without me right
                                in front of me stomata
Also open   optimize   speak
                                        if speech
Equilibrates   uncurls   and causes
                                        modestly
To prosper

0

Epithalamium

                                                    Then spring
returns,   or never left, since all is spring returning stress
applied to it, a hand restoring force   to pinions hidden
in a bonnet of mahogany that push the pallet fork and spur
the sun and smiling moon   and sun again to cross
the mind of time behind a brow   of glass, no mind easier
than time's to read. The day is clear   before it's torsion
-shorn of bonds that whipsaw thunderheads   from crystal
clarity, an open field   of permittivity, each flower filled with
leaping bee   + not to be, a quantum trill the wood-thrush
sings in subsong with itself. A song that keeps collapsing,

wave into a particle, particular, the world as it is   caught
in glimpses being   built before my eyes as I drive west,
the overpass beside the Pfizer plant raised up on pillars
in the air, a span   of still-soft silicate. A bridge of calcium
exists between each   synapse thinking all the other ways
this could have gone, remembering a summer years ago
returning to a stream beneath the interchange to listen
to the seams absorb a double   knock of axles front and rear
traversing   intervals. The feeling was   of being in, inside,

yet hurtling   at speed through leaves of gold, an α particle
discharged to shadow   forth the orbitals of spin and probability
that clot   into the adamant undappled shade of dog- and
arrowwood down disused gravel lanes, each route burnt,
not taking it, behind my eyes, so when I slept I dreamed
of tunneling for years through August heat, the roads
eroding into scree that falls away to bare a bone of bluestone
shouldered underneath. Since then I've sought for something less

than groundedness, less a shifting earth as much as shifting
to account for it, its sprawling grids and parishes refolding
into anamorphic plumb. The land a sudden death's head
falling   into place along an axis threading smoothbore
balls of brass that spindle in and out of overlap, or molecules
in graphic laddering, in 3D-rendered images of silicon
and oxygen I click   and drag until the mesh resolves

an openwork that indicates the angle quartz is cut to rectify
the current worming through its structured starch. A second,

split, if time   is crystalline, in which we felt the opposite of slow
collapse while crossing fields that fill   the razed perimeter
of Sanford Cotton Mill   to climb inside the ruined campanile
that housed the shaft for hauling bales from floor
to floor. Above, the crossbars giving rung to rain, a hoist
wheel hangs   a kind of bell, but less for keeping time than
straining to avoid this   graceless plunge, a plangent upswung
song instead that stalls against the well in space the planet makes.
But song   is always sung too late, the tuning slips,
then slips again, the gear spurs stripped, and synchrony unspools

an apple from its skin or sun   unspun on threaded screw
into a wormhole coring through   itself, achieving
such a density it breaches worlds as easily   as low stone walls
are overstepped, a knotted fruit   on either side we leave
to rot or came   too late to save from sunkenness and wasps.
Our carelessness, this   lateness now   our only shared reality,
a field   in staggered synthesis with field, disparity   if not
resolved then held   in tension as the advent of dimension,
depth, a crystal focus in the seamless   steepled air the morning
of our wedding hunting   chamomile in pastures near
the interstate   you later press between anthologies of poetry,
the heaviest we own, to form a wreath to bind us to the earth
in close array, a nearly   spaceless petaling of planes
and lattices in lancets flensing interference from a pip

of copper sulfide feathered on a pin. The light diffracted
in a hive or net is also evidence that what was thought
discrete and bright and singular   as juniper unfolds a wave
of world   on world. All solidness, its granulets
of birefringent myelin, the precondition for discovery
of underlying chanciness, all chancelry   established
on a Burgess Shale of everything   that could have been. The earth
a thin accumulated dust   on petals in a bowl, and what is earth
there for except   to unconceal each spring the cold
white crocus in the woods, its ceaseless oscillations   slowed
into the momentary openness   appearance is? A bud
that pops in place, then out, the downswing of a metronome

or leaden sinker dropped into an unclenched fist, the present
for an instant in the loosened freshet   of my grip, then pulled,

and with it ripped   the muscles in my palm, the spring
of what I thought I held   recoiling, time-kept, time-reeled
-back, arm in arcing hides its fleeting hand   -tied fly upstream,
the song   unhanding me, and then with equal even
-handedness comes axing back, an apsis dragging with it
supermoons in perigee: the world brought near again,
where world is always   what I least expect, but recognize
as mine, all this   time, a second chance to keep
the promises I made   made dear in retrograde, this
backward step I take   to you, bell-like, swung   so that the tongue
is always catching up, and speaks its alternating oath of late
and soon on both the east   and western rim of bronze, each
day a tune that goes *this   time this   time this   time* as if

                                        this time

                        it might be true

Notes

[anyte]: incorporates two quotations—one from *The Confessions* by Saint Augustine, as found in *Lyric Time: Dickinson and the Limits of Genre* by Sharon Cameron, and one from *Helen in Egypt* by H.D.

[a garland of souls]: incorporates a quotation from Book 11 of *The Paradiso* by Dante Alighieri, trans. John Ciardi.

[eros / eris]: samples language from "Compensation" by Ralph Waldo Emerson.

Fidelity: samples language from *The Garden of Cyrus* by Sir Thomas Browne.

Helen: samples two lines from poems in *Mulberry* and *Circle's Apprentice* by Dan Beachy-Quick and manipulates language found in "Oread" by H.D. and "Rings" by Pinegrove. *Terres labourées* (1999) is a painting by Pietro Sarto. Other companion texts include the *Cantos* by Ezra Pound, the *Four Quartets* by T. S. Eliot, "Hyperion: A Fragment" by John Keats, and *Catalogue d'oiseaux* by Aaron Tucker.

Anabasis: invokes Gerard Manley Hopkins, T. S. Eliot, and "[With the voice of the fieldmouse]" by Paul Celan.

levity [rage is also prone to structure]: invokes H.D., Emily Dickinson, Robert Duncan, and Wallace Stevens.

levity [structure as a form of rage itself]: alludes to a "death-hyacinth" mentioned in *Palimpsest* by H.D.

levity [as gun-heavy]: draws inspiration from "'Fire is one...'" by John Peck.

levity [life in this world the other's catastrophe]: manipulates language found in "Canto 74" from the *Cantos* by Ezra Pound.

levity [where desire was was edge]: alludes to "Hermes of the Ways" by H.D., a loose translation or transposition of a poem by Anyte of Tegea, and to "In a Station of the Metro" by Ezra Pound. It also alludes to a battle-scene in Book 4 of Homer's *Iliad*.

Redux: alludes to "I felt a Funeral, in my Brain" (M 179) by Emily Dickinson. It samples a short phrase from "Caños de Meca" by Toby Martinez de las Rivas.

Shield or bee: alludes to a letter from Rainer Maria Rilke to Witold Hulewicz, November 13, 1925.

35°43'00.5"N 75°29'29.5"W: alludes to "Canto 116" from the *Cantos* by Ezra Pound.

35°45'53.5"N 79°12'01.8"W: alludes to "Often I am Permitted to Return to a Meadow" by Robert Duncan.

35°54'05.4"N 78°50'45.2"W: manipulates language found in *The Ethics of the Dust* by John Ruskin and "Split the Lark – and you'll find the music" (M 427) by Emily Dickinson. It also alludes to "Canto 4" from the *Cantos* by Ezra Pound.

35°59'49.1"N 78°54'11.1"W: alludes to "To Autumn" by John Keats and *The Walls Do Not Fall* by H.D.

Gnat brain: samples language from "Ozymandias" by Percy Bysshe Shelley, the epigraph to *Hugh Selwyn Mauberley* by Ezra Pound, a journal entry for December 22, 1837, by Henry David Thoreau, and "'The Oracular Tree Acquiring': On Romanticism as Radical Praxis" by Dan Beachy-Quick.

Axis: alludes to Book 9, XVIII in *The Confucian Analects,* trans. Ezra Pound.

Tongue-tie: is for Zora Dekeersgieter.

Pitkin / Column: alludes to "The Church and the Laws of the Land" by Charles W. Nibley, "Sea Lily" by H.D., and "Gifts" by Ralph Waldo Emerson.

A vision: invokes Frances Sargent Osgood and incorporates language from "Mary Had a Little Lamb" by Sarah Josepha Hale. It also alludes to "The Noble Rider and the Sound of Words" by Wallace Stevens.

Epithalamium: draws inspiration from "Wedge" by G.C. Waldrep and "ε: A Small, Positive Quantity" by Colin Dekeersgieter. Other companion texts include *Crystal Fire: The Birth of the Information Age* by Michael Riordan and Lillian Hoddeson, the *Four Quartets* by Eliot, and *Orrery* and *The Invention of the Zero* by Richard Kenney. The opening lines allude to the eighteenth-century Dutch thinker François Hemsterhuis and his sense that "all is spring."

Acknowledgments

Thanks to *Annulet: A Journal of Poetics, Bennington Review, Brink, Colorado Review, The Decadent Review, Denver Quarterly, Oxidant | Engine, Quarterly West, Seneca Review,* and *Under a Warm Green Linden* for publishing some of the poems from this book.

Special thanks are also due to Dan Beachy-Quick, Colin Dekeersgieter, Karah Mitchell, and Eliza Richards. Many thanks, too, to David Blakesley for his editorial vision and support.

My deepest gratitude goes to Jon Thompson, both for believing in this book and for his generosity as a friend and editor.

About the Author

Kylan Rice is the author of *Incryptions*, a collection of essays. He is co-author of *Primer*, a collection of conversations with the poet Dan Beachy-Quick, and co-editor of *Southern Lights: 75 Years of the Carolina Quarterly*. His poems and essays have appeared in *Colorado Review, Denver Quarterly, Image, Kenyon Review Online*, and *West Branch*, among other journals. He is the associate editor of the *Missouri Review*.

Photograph of the author by Elizabeth Poindexter. Used by permission.

Free Verse Editions

Edited by Jon Thompson

13 ways of happily by Emily Carr
& in Open, Marvel by Felicia Zamora
& there's you still thrill hour of the world to love by Aby Kaupang
Alias by Eric Pankey
the atmosphere is not a perfume it is odorless by Matthew Cooperman
At Your Feet (A Teus Pés) by Ana Cristina César, edited by Katrina Dodson, trans. by Brenda Hillman and Helen Hillman
Bari's Love Song by Kang Eun-Gyo, translated by Chung Eun-Gwi
Between the Twilight and the Sky by Jennie Neighbors
Blood Orbits by Ger Killeen
The Bodies by Christopher Sindt
The Book of Isaac by Aidan Semmens
The Calling by Bruce Bond
Canticle of the Night Path by Jennifer Atkinson
Child in the Road by Cindy Savett
Civil Twilight by Giles Goodland
Condominium of the Flesh by Valerio Magrelli, trans. by Clarissa Botsford
Contrapuntal by Christopher Kondrich
Country Album by James Capozzi
Cry Baby Mystic by Daniel Tiffany
The Curiosities by Brittany Perham
Current by Lisa Fishman
Day In, Day Out by Simon Smith
Dear Reader by Bruce Bond
Dismantling the Angel by Eric Pankey
Divination Machine by F. Daniel Rzicznek
Elsewhere, That Small by Monica Berlin
Empire by Tracy Zeman
Erros by Morgan Lucas Schuldt
Extinction of the Holy City by Bronisław Maj, trans. by Daniel Bourne
Fifteen Seconds without Sorrow by Shim Bo-Seon, trans. by Chung Eun-Gwi and Brother Anthony of Taizé
The Forever Notes by Ethel Rackin
The Flying House by Dawn-Michelle Baude
General Release from the Beginning of the World by Donna Spruijt-Metz
Ghost Letters by Baba Badji
Go On by Ethel Rackin
Here City by Rick Snyder
An Image Not a Book by Kylan Rice

An Unchanging Blue: Selected Poems 1962–1975 by Rolf Dieter Brinkmann, trans. by Mark Terrill

Under the Quick by Molly Bendall

Verge by Morgan Lucas Schuldt

The Visible Woman by Allison Funk

The Wash by Adam Clay

Well by Sasha Steensen

We'll See by Georges Godeau, trans. by Kathleen McGookey

What Stillness Illuminated by Yermiyahu Ahron Taub

Winter Journey [Viaggio d'inverno] by Attilio Bertolucci, trans. by Nicholas Benson

Wonder Rooms by Allison Funk

www.ingramcontent.com/pod-product-compliance
Lightning Source LLC
Chambersburg PA
CBHW031147090426
42738CB00008B/1252